LAKE TROUT

SMALLMOUTH BASS

YELLOW PERCH

FRESHWATER GAME FISH
of NORTH AMERICA

To the scientists and educators committed to protecting the Great Lakes —B.R.

For Brad —J.C.

Special thanks to Cindy Hudson, Brandon Schroeder, Meaghan Gass (Michigan Sea Grant), and Dr. Jeff Reutter (retired director, Ohio Sea Grant/Stone Lab) for their extensive comments on text and art. Thanks to Sea Grant educators Terri Hallesy, Prabhjot Singh Chawla (Illinois/Indiana), Emily Jones (Minnesota), Lyndsey Manzo (Ohio), Ginny Carlton, Anne Moser (Wisconsin), Michelle Niedermeier (Pennsylvania), and Nate Drag (New York) for their review. For specific answers, I thank Kathleen Smith, Great Lakes Indian Fish & Wildlife Commission; Dr. Lauren Fry, Jennifer Day, Margaret Lansing, NOAA; Dr. Patty Loew, Inaugural Director, Center for Native American and Indigenous Research, Northwestern University; Jennifer Caddick, Beth Amatangelo, Alliance for the Great Lakes; Jillian Votava, Inland Seas Education Association; Dr. John W. Johnston, University of Waterloo; Dr. Jim Selegean, U.S. Army Corps of Engineers; Heather Hahn Sullivan, Dunes Learning Center; and Paul Labovitz, Kim Swift, Dan Plath, National Park Service.

THE GREAT LAKES

OUR FRESHWATER TREASURE

By **Barb Rosenstock**

Illustrated by **Jamey Christoph**

ALFRED A. KNOPF 🐕 NEW YORK

CANADA

UNITED STATES
OF AMERICA

MEXICO

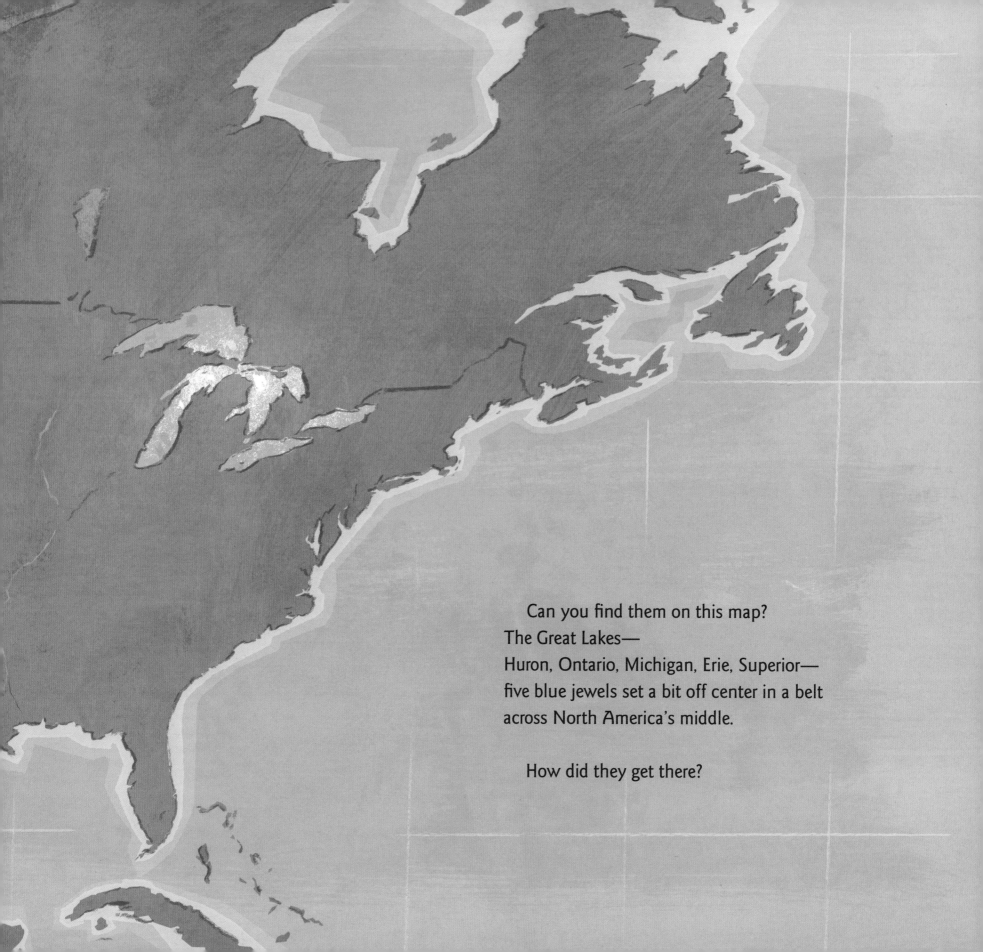

Can you find them on this map?
The Great Lakes—
Huron, Ontario, Michigan, Erie, Superior—
five blue jewels set a bit off center in a belt
across North America's middle.

How did they get there?

It all started with snowflakes, a LOT of snowflakes.

About two million years ago, the Earth tilted, and this part of the globe wound up a bit farther from the sun. It was cold all the time.

If you were a snowflake back then, you were in luck! You didn't melt. Neither did many of your fellow flakes, even in summer. Zillions of you piled up year after year and packed into ice. This ice formed a glacier— the biggest ever known.

This glacier covered five million square miles, more than half of North America! It was super tall—like ten skyscrapers piled atop one another—about two miles thick in some places. And super heavy, pressing the land's surface down a skyscraper deep, at least eight hundred feet.

The colder it got, the more the ice built up and pushed the glacier forward. If it warmed a bit, the ice melted and the glacier pulled back. Colder, forward. Warmer, back. Scouring the land for hundreds of thousands of years. Tumbling trees. Pulverizing rocks. Digging holes.

A million or so years later, the Earth tilted again, and this part of the globe returned closer to the sun. *Whoosh!* The glacier melted. Its water was trapped in five glacier-dug holes. As the weight of the ice was removed, thawing land rose all around. The Great Lakes were born.

Like growing children, the Great Lakes changed size and shape. For thousands of years, their boundaries shifted—north, south, east, and west. A dynamic mix of waterways fed and drained their basins.

Thundering storms, furious blizzards, battering waves, and shifting winds

created a wealth of rare dunes,

timeless forests, and limestone cliffs.

Under the water, meadows of wild celery and curly pondweed swayed. Microscopic diatoms fed plankton, worms, and crustaceans. These tiny creatures fattened 139 native species of fish, including perch, trout, walleye . . .

. . . and a fish as big as a very big person—the bony-plated lake sturgeon. It can grow seven feet long, weigh as much as two hundred pounds, and live more than one hundred years.

The Great Lakes took their current shape only three thousand years ago. They're the youngest major geological feature on the planet—millions of years younger than the Appalachian Mountains, the Great Plains, and the Mississippi River. They keep changing today. Storms move shorelines and sand dunes. Land rebounding from the glacier's weight rises. Rocks wear down as lake levels surge and fall. Still, the water flows on, west to east.

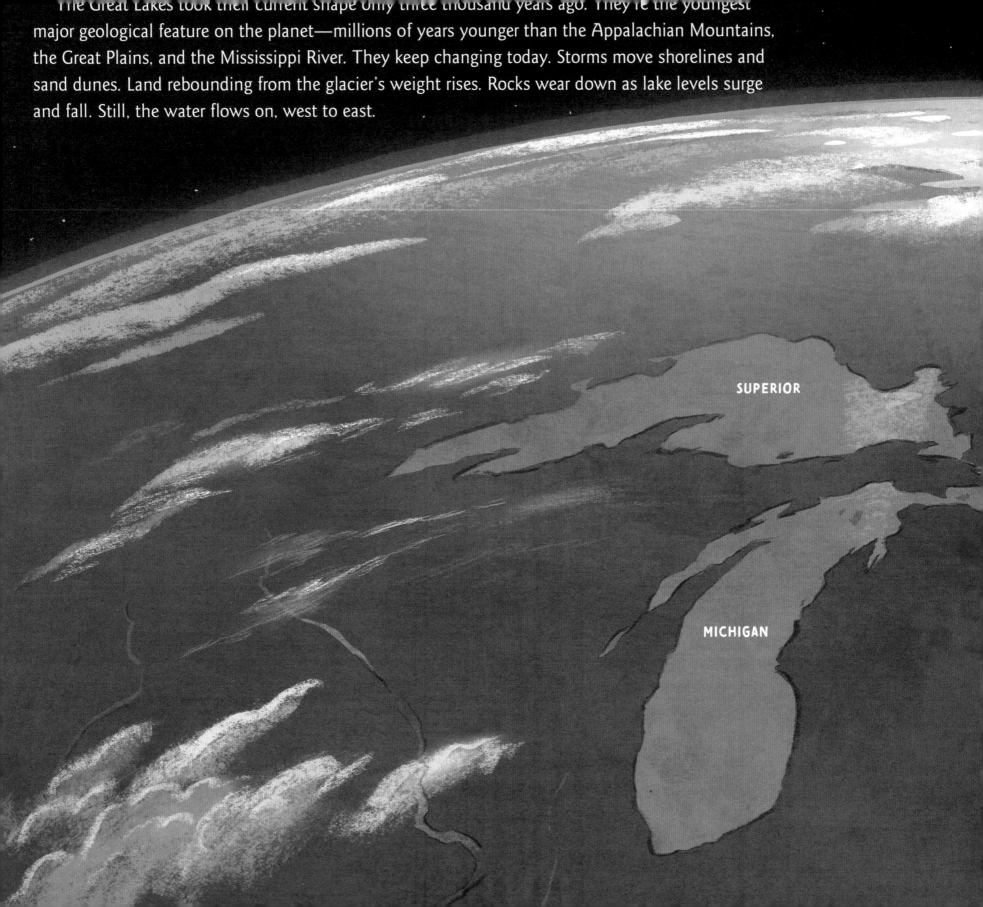

SUPERIOR

MICHIGAN

THE GREAT LAKES IN PROFILE

LAKE ERIE
(210 FT.)

NIAGARA FALLS

LAKE HURON
(750 FT.)

LAKE MICHIGAN
(923 FT.)

ST. LAWRENCE RIVER

LAKE ONTARIO
(802 FT.)

ATLANTIC OCEAN

LAKE SUPERIOR
(1,330 FT.)

(MAXIMUM DEPTH IN FEET)

Because all five Great Lakes connect—working together like a single stair-stepped river.

HURON

ONTARIO

ERIE

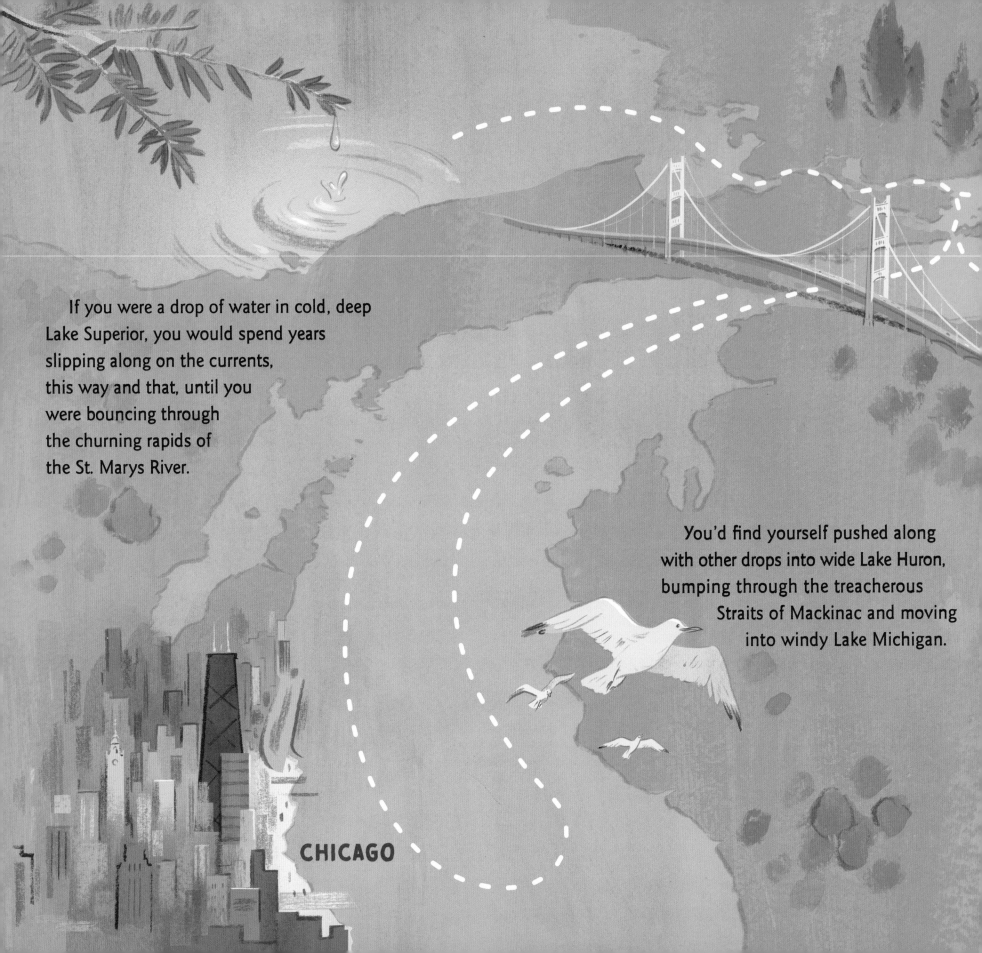

If you were a drop of water in cold, deep Lake Superior, you would spend years slipping along on the currents, this way and that, until you were bouncing through the churning rapids of the St. Marys River.

You'd find yourself pushed along with other drops into wide Lake Huron, bumping through the treacherous Straits of Mackinac and moving into windy Lake Michigan.

CHICAGO

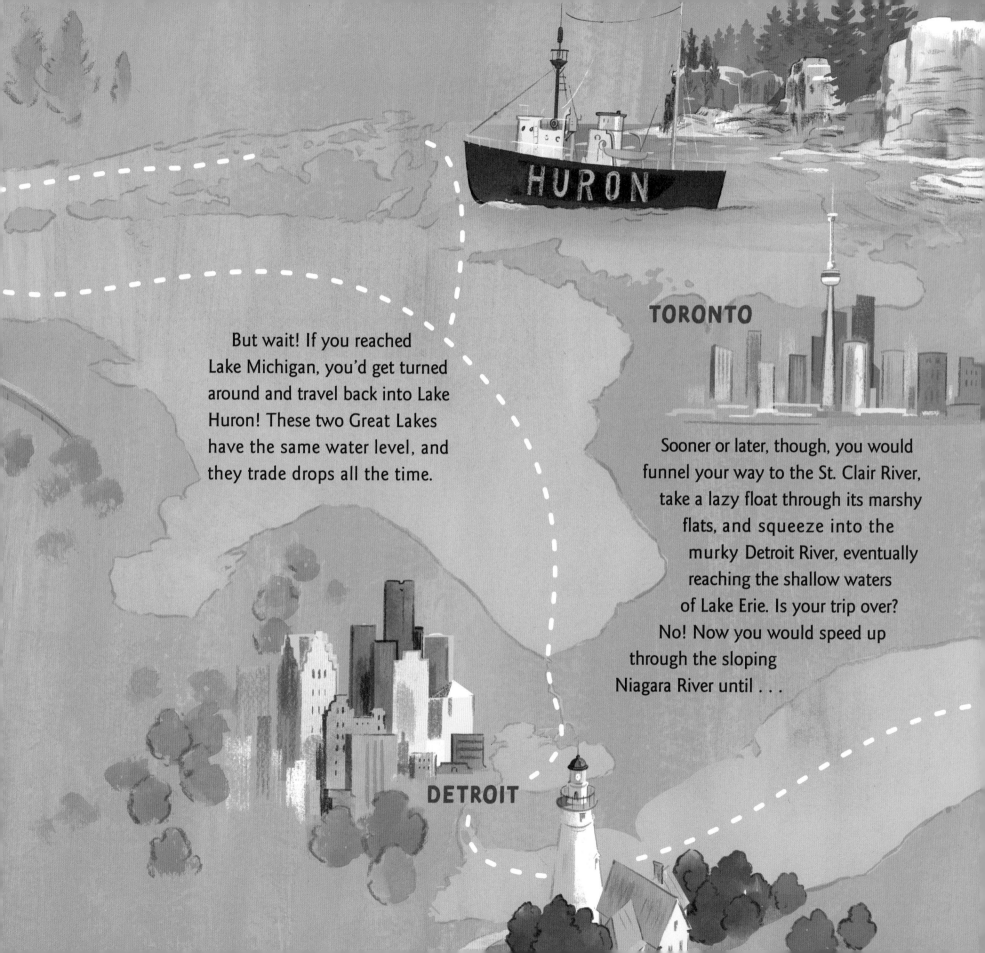

HURON

TORONTO

But wait! If you reached Lake Michigan, you'd get turned around and travel back into Lake Huron! These two Great Lakes have the same water level, and they trade drops all the time.

Sooner or later, though, you would funnel your way to the St. Clair River, take a lazy float through its marshy flats, and squeeze into the murky Detroit River, eventually reaching the shallow waters of Lake Erie. Is your trip over? No! Now you would speed up through the sloping Niagara River until . . .

DETROIT

Niagara FALLS!

You're one drop in a LOT of drops—about 54 million drops! Part of three thousand tons of Great Lakes water plunging over the falls each second.

Splash! You would dive into narrow Lake Ontario and tour around thousands of islands in the St. Lawrence River. Until, at last, you and the other freshwater drops mix with the salty drops that make up the Atlantic Ocean. Your trip passes by the longest coastline in the mainland United States—4,530 miles, more than the Atlantic and Pacific coasts combined. Guess how long that trip takes the average drop? About three hundred years!

The Great Lakes hold six quadrillion gallons of water—that's 6,000,000,000,000,000. If the Great Lakes ever spilled over the land, everyone in North America would be swimming in water five feet deep.

LAKE AVE

Still, that's not much compared to the entire planet. The Earth is covered in water, a LOT of water—326 quintillion gallons. That's 326,000,000,000,000,000,000,000.
What makes Great Lakes water so special?

Imagine that one hundred bottles contain all of the Earth's water. Thirsty? Hope not. Ninety-seven bottles are saltwater, mostly from the oceans. Undrinkable. Two bottles are freshwater, but they're frozen solid, locked mostly in polar ice.

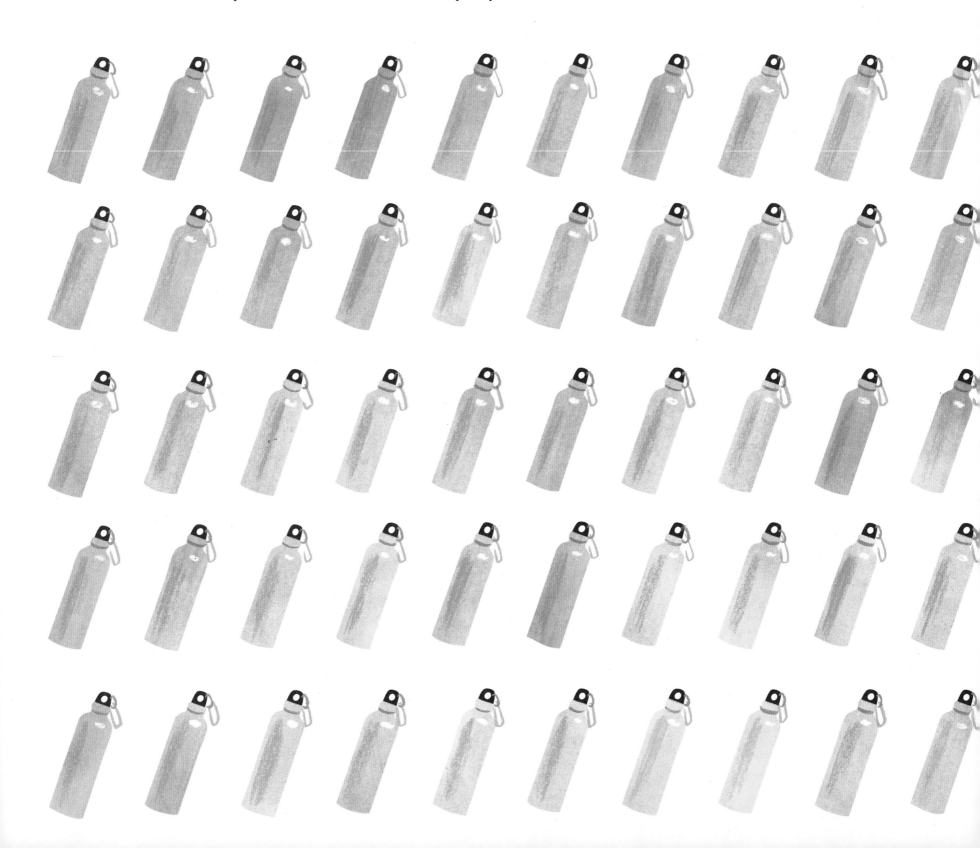

If you were a bottle of liquid freshwater, you'd be the only one! On the planet. And every living thing wants a sip. *Gulp!* Most of this freshwater is stuck underground, hard to reach. Only a fraction is on Earth's surface.

And wow, do people use it!

If you were a person . . .

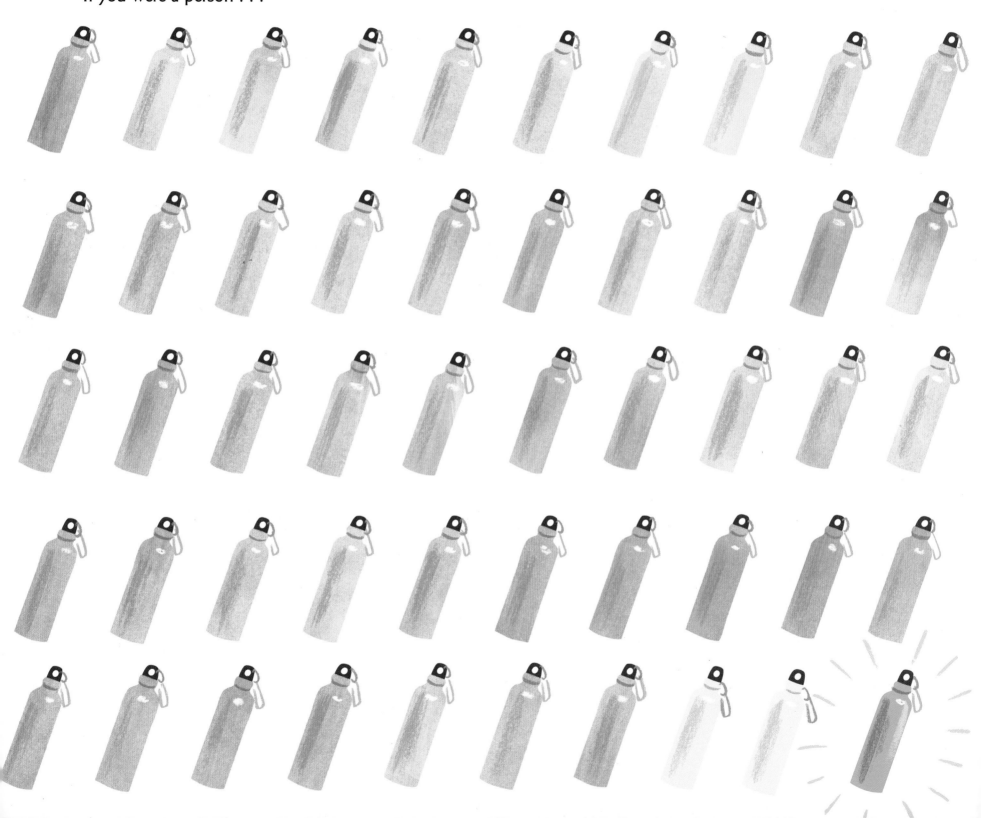

Wait! You *are* a person! So, you probably use surface freshwater every day for drinking, washing, or playing.

This water grows the food you eat, cooks it, and rinses the dishes.

Surface freshwater runs factories, transports cargo, even creates electricity.
It makes up three quarters of the water used in the United States.

Where does much of this precious water come from? The Great Lakes! They contain almost all of the surface freshwater on the North American continent. One in every five glasses of the surface freshwater on Earth!

LAKE SUPERIOR

LAKE MICHIGAN

LAKE ONTARIO

LAKE HURON

LAKE ERIE

For thousands of years, Native peoples harvested the
Great Lakes' rich resources, using only what they needed.

But a few hundred years ago, Europeans settled in the Great Lakes region and started overusing the resources. They took more than they needed, more and more every year.

People cleared forests, overfished waters,

drained swamps, farmed wetlands, dug canals and seaways, constructed cities, and built huge factories.

The Great Lakes struggled. Unshaded waters grew warmer, dozens of invasive plants and animals moved in, many native plants and animals died off, dangerous chemicals swirled and settled in the lake beds.

When the Great Lakes' shining water started turning to sludge, finally, people changed. They began to protest pollution, preserve shoreline, protect plants and animals. More people spoke up for the Great Lakes, more and more every year. Some chemicals were cleaned up, some trees grew back, some creatures returned. More needs to be done. How can you help?

The same way we can all help.
By caring for wild places. By working with groups that protect the lakes.
And by saving freshwater, wherever we are, whenever we can.

Then the Great Lakes—
Huron, Ontario, Michigan, Erie, Superior—
those five blue jewels set a bit off center in a belt
across North America's middle,
have the chance
to remain a great treasure,
for you, for all of us, forever.

A Message from a Great Lakes Caretaker

To All Our Relatives of Mother Earth,

Gichigami (the Great Sea) is a special place. In Anishinaabe culture, it was there at the beginning of time. In our tradition, Gichi-manidoo (the Great Mystery) formed Mother Earth through the four orders of creation. The first order is the elements—fire, water, earth, and air. The second order is the plants. The third order is the animals, and the fourth order is humans. As a people, we depend on each order; each order does not depend on us. All things have a spirit. Each element, each plant, each animal, and each human being. The life-giving element that connects us all is nibi (water).

For the Ojibwe people, the Great Sea is also our migration route, from the Atlantic Ocean to the Great Lakes. In our migration story, we were told to head where the food grows on the water. We use the beautiful gifts that Mother Earth offers us, manoomin (wild rice) and giigoonh (fish), as food in our culture and ceremonies.

We have much work ahead of us to help Mother Earth and her life-giving nibi. We honor our beautiful Earth and the Great Lakes by singing to the water, respecting the water, and showing the water how much we care. When we are good caretakers, in turn, nibi will take care of us. The Great Lakes provide the freshest water system to millions of people. We can be good helpers by keeping nibi and the beaches clean. We can also do our part by saying gaawiin (no) to plastic. For instance, we can start with reusable water bottles.

We need to be a good relative to the water to help it stay clean for children like you, and for future generations of children, too.

Wasanodaekwe (Northern Lights Woman)
Ma'iingan indoodem (wolf clan) of wiikwedong indoonjibaa (a place along the water)
Kathleen Smith
Genawendang Manoomin
"She who takes care of the wild rice"
Great Lakes Indian Fish & Wildlife Commission
Enrolled member, Keweenaw Bay Indian Community

Great Lakes Literacy

How can you help the Great Lakes?

The Center for Great Lakes Literacy engages and inspires students, teachers, and scientists to promote improved stewardship of our shared freshwater treasure. The Center—through its Sea Grant educators and resources located throughout the watershed—helps teachers and youth explore the Great Lakes through education and stewardship opportunities in their own schools and communities! Learn more about the Center for Great Lakes Literacy at cgll.org.

CENTER FOR
CGLL
GREAT LAKES LITERACY

Author's Note

A treasure is something rare and valuable. It's something we keep safe, and if we decide to spend a portion, we must do so wisely.

Lake Michigan is my home, the setting of my personal story. I have lived within fifteen miles of its borders my entire life. As a young girl, I played in its watershed creeks; as a young woman, I watched lake storms from a high-rise window. Today, I grow my suburban garden with its plentiful water. Still, before researching this book, I did not know that the Great Lakes are considered "the continent's most valuable resource."[1]

As a region and a topic, the Great Lakes are so BIG! In this book, I've covered less than a millionth of the geology, hydrology, meteorology, biology, and other scientific subjects that explain the entire Great Lakes system. I did not detail human history, industry, or many environmental challenges. It would take hundreds of books to tell the whole story.

Today, one in ten people in the United States live in the Great Lakes region, along with one in three Canadians—almost 50 million people. Since the human body is about 60 percent water, if you are one of the millions of kids who get their drinking water from the Great Lakes, in a very real sense, you ARE the Great Lakes. That drinking water is pumped, cleaned, used, treated, and mostly returned, for now. As population grows and the climate warms, freshwater—already scarce around the globe—will become even more scarce in North America.

The Great Lakes are jointly governed by eight states in the United States, plus two Canadian provinces. Federal and tribal governments, universities, and hundreds of organizations work on Great Lakes conservation. Some pressing issues include pollution from mining, logging close to shorelines, potential leakage from aging oil pipelines, and continued threats from invasive species. Plans have been proposed to pipe Great Lakes water to desert areas or bottle and sell it to other countries. Difficult decisions must be made. Our water conservation actions, individually and together, make a difference. Cooperation, education, and activism are important to guard the future of these great treasures.

1. Folger, Tim. *National Geographic*, Dec. 2020, p. 41.

Selected Sources

Alliance for the Great Lakes. *Great Lakes in My World* (K–8 curriculum). Chicago: Alliance for the Great Lakes, 2005.

Ashworth, William. *The Late, Great Lakes: An Environmental History.* Detroit: Wayne State University Press, 1986.

Bornhorst, Theodore J. "An Overview of the Geology of the Great Lakes Basin." A. E. Seaman Mineral Museum of Michigan Tech, 2016.
museum.mtu.edu/sites/default/files/2019-11/AESMM_Web_Pub_1_Great_Lakes_Geology_0.pdf

Dennis, Jerry. *The Living Great Lakes: Searching for the Heart of the Inland Seas.* New York: St. Martin's Press, 2003.

Dietz, Thomas, and David Bidwell. *Climate Change in the Great Lakes Region: Navigating an Uncertain Future.* East Lansing: Michigan State University Press, 2012.

Egan, Dan. *The Death and Life of the Great Lakes.* New York: W. W. Norton, 2017.

Folger, Tim. "North America's Most Valuable Resource Is at Risk." *National Geographic*, v. December 2020 (Issue titled "Saving the Great Lakes").

Grady, Wayne. *The Great Lakes: The Natural History of a Changing Region.* Vancouver: Greystone Books, 2007.

greatlakesseagrant.com

Mortimer, Clifford H. "Props and Actors on a Massive Stage." Chapter 1 of *The Enduring Great Lakes: A Natural History Book.* John Rousmaniere (ed.). New York: W. W. Norton, 1979. noaa.gov

Schloesser, Donald W. *A Field Guide to Valuable Underwater Aquatic Plants of the Great Lakes.* U.S. Fish and Wildlife Service. Ann Arbor: Great Lakes Fishery Laboratory, 1986.

U.S. Environmental Protection Agency and the Government of Canada. *The Great Lakes: An Environmental Atlas and Resource Book.* Third Edition, 1995.

RIVER

FOREST

ESTUARY

DELTA

DELTA

LAKE

SAVING LIFE SERVICE U.S.